VISIONS FUGITIVE

Visions Fugitive

Ralph Gustafson

PREFACE BY BRUCE WHITEMAN

Véhicule Press

MONTRÉAL

Published with the assistance of the Canada Council.

Cover art and design by Mark Garland.
Photograph of the author by Betty Gustafson.
Typeset in Perpetua by Simon Garamond.
Printed by Imprimerie d'Édition Marquis Ltée.
Special thanks to Bruce Whiteman.

CANADIAN CATALOGUING IN PUBLICATION DATA

Gustafson, Ralph 1909-1995
Visions fugitive

Poems.
ISBN 1-55065-081-5

I. Title
PS8513.U7V56 1996   C811'.54   C96-900462-1
PR9199.3.G8V48 1996

Published by Véhicule Press
P.O.B. 125, Place du Parc Station,
Montreal, Quebec, Canada H2W 2M9
http://www.cam.org/~vpress

Distributed by General Distribution Services
30 Lesmill Rd., Don Mills, Ontario M3B 2T6

Printed in Canada on alkaline paper.

for Betty

And the sun shall rise
And be as a grace.

—*Winter Prophecies*

Contents

Preface

Visions Fugitive is Ralph Gustafson's last book of poems, completed not long before his death in May, 1995. While it was in progress he referred to it as "More Unread Poems," an uncharacteristically direct admission of his frustration with his place in the world of poetry and with poetry's place in the world. Illness spoke in that unhappiness, atypically for Ralph, who had come through close battles with mortality more than once before without spiritual depletion. Like many of his friends I refrained from advising him not to stick with so bare and pessimistic a title in the hope that it was only provisional. So in fact it was, and eventually he settled on *Visions Fugitive*, a resonant choice in many ways, the obeisance to Prokofiev and his piano pieces of the same name not least among them.

As he entered the last decade of his life, with *Directives of Autumn* (1984) Ralph published the first of four books—the others were *Winter Prophecies* (1987), *Shadows in the Grass* (1991), and *Tracks in the Snow* (1994)—that are dominated by images of fall and winter and that wrestle determinately with the great questions of the end of life: death, God, evil, and the absolute joy and passion of being alive. "The endless search, question," begins "Wheel of Fire," the first poem in *Directives of Autumn*, with its Shakespearean title and its characteristically Gustafsonesque description of the earth as "astringent and sweet." If in one sense it is perfectly easy to see the world that way—the horror and the glory of it—in another, for a poet, it is immensely demanding to hold that paradox in focus through poem after poem, book after book. It was part of Ralph's deep humanity and his greatness as a poet that he was able to do just that, never to give in to execration or sentimentality, however attractive each sometimes is. The other book of that last decade, the autobiographical *Configurations at Midnight* (1992), ends with the line "Sensation claims me, I leave my love," as beautiful, ambiguous, and heart-breaking a resolution of the paradox that is the world as I can imagine.

Visons Fugitive provides no definite answers to the questions Ralph posed again and again through his late books. He knew that the questions were unanswerable anyway, that in a deep sense the life of the mind and the life of the body depend on the creative tension produced by irresolution and the imponderable. Perhaps the tone in this final book is more sombre than usual, despite the epigraph ("And the sun shall rise / And be as a grace") and the discovery that persistance itself is a kind of redemption ("Meditation About Being Continuous"). The opening travel poems lack Ralph's usual joy at visiting foreign places, and the hospital poems that conclude the collection leave us with images of illness and unbelief. That is fair enough, though it represents a far different cast of mind from the few evidences in the book of Ralph's more usual relish ("No, it won't do, extinction, / Inevitable impoverishment, I won't accept it—"). Even poetry itself, long the most essential of Ralph's carrion comforts, is mostly absent as a subject; and behind his brief "In Memoriam" for E.J. Pratt ("For a Poet") I cannot help but hear a *clamabo* for himself ("What did it get you, old friend? / Erasure.").

The poems in *Visions Fugitive* do not testify directly to any foreknowledge Ralph might have had that this would be his last book. There are bits of the private past re-remembered vividly here and there (his first date with Betty, his wife-to-be, for example, in "What Happened") as well as fragmentary notes of teleological confession in phrases like "Eden, an offhand / Prohibition" or "The world / Worse, ourselves unreconciled." But only the final few poems seem to tip over into a slightly grim withdrawal from the world, a place which his last few books never entered, for all their concern with the great themes of old age. Certainly "One dies / unfinished," as Ralph has it in "The Lurking Abyss"; but up to that final point his love of life is as acute as ever, as poems like "Sensualities" and "Each Knows of It" show.

It is unfair to whittle a poet's work of a lifetime down to a representative poem, much less a single line; but I have long thought that the opening line of Ralph's poem "Winter Prophecies" encapsulated much of what his poetry is about: "Beyond all wisdom is the lonely heart." There is wisdom in this last book, as always, for Ralph was an infinitely wise poet. Yet finally it is the lonely heart which predominates, by itself as the heart always must be, contemplating life and death and solitude, in love but ultimately unrequited, and beautifully articulate.

Bruce Whiteman
Montreal, March 9-10, 1996

Sardonics

NEWS

The youngster with the old woman scrounges
The pockets of snow for bark, shreddings,
Sticks for fire; for the sniper in the hills
The light is still good, hate
Available.

      We found Belgrade dull
But that was years back. The walls
Of Dubrovnik were much livelier, my wife
Found the embroidery sold below
The steep barbican excellent. The city
Was worth the loss of the sapphire—
Down the drain of the bathtub, the setting
Of her ring was loose—the swimmers naked
On the coastal rocks a habit known
Throughout Europe. Sarajevo then
Was where they shot the Hapsburg duke,
Then of the memorable Olympic Games.

SARAJEVO 1994

Of love lying across the dead, I mourn,
She of the Muslim faith, he in the strangeness
Of his Christian death, the aim from the sniper finer.

Six days they lay partway across
The Miljacka bridge, the sanitary detail held up...

The usual smell invested the rotting bodies—
But that was not it. One covered his nostrils—
Hate from the bodies came off.

HATE

How shall the heart commend·this,
Barbed wire to be remembered?

                Israeli, Arab,
                       worship
At the tomb of Abraham of Ur.
                Goodness
Gives the United Nations concern.

Milosevic picks his crucifixions,
Zhirinovsky sucks his teeth.

PETRARCH 1995

How Croats themselves were massacred
Who had massacred Serbs … I put by the book,
Listened to the disc I had put on the player,
Liszt's setting of the 104th
Of Petrarch's Sonnets of Love. "Warfare
I cannot wage yet know not peace."
The newly-bound signatures drew back
On the spine. "I grasp the whole world
Yet nothing can obtain." History!
I shut the book.

A FURTHER HALF-DOZEN LINES

Still the resonance comes—under
The chandeliers, the statistician's
Dissections, the ghetto's dimensions, history
In error. The halls are brilliant, tribal
Assertion is a nation, mopping up
Is preferable

And ewes and jackals.

HAPPY VALENTINE

Statistics are reality. 5%
Of the Western population wear
Prostheses. 10% of Cessna pilots
Are colour-blind. 80%
Of the world's politicians are elected
By illiterate voters.
98% of the quota impositions
Stabilize commonality.
Presently 1.4 children
Are born to each woman in China.

    The message is clear,
    We must love one another 1.6%.

AT THE CASTALIAN SPRING

Reality is virtual. We sat beside
Castalian waters that year
At Delphi where trees of olives
Sequester Apollo the god of healing's
Oracle. We sat with assorted tourists
On what was left of the marble steps.
Below, in the valley, the Crissean temple
Stumbled to ruin. The hot sun sang,
The crickets chirred, the guide talked.
In the Gallery the bronze charioteer
Drove his horses to victorious war.
We were attentive, heard how Pythia
On her tripod in the cleft of rock
Prophesied what was to come,
Her gibberish picked over by lobbying priests.

        Back to Athens, just
        Acceptably polluted.
        Next day to Egypt, proprietor
        Of resplendent graves.

MADRID MIDDAY

The hot Spanish sun was over the city,
The midday traffic circled the square.
My wife was taking my picture, the statue
Of Cervantes on the tablature behind me.
"Get off the grass!" the keeper of the square
Yelled at me. "It's Don Quixote's! Vamos!"
We did. The man continued clipping.
The snapshot came out but little
Of the perspective. Trafalgar lay
Ahead. I had had it, picadors,
Parrots and corncob cathedral.
Cervantes is right. No delusion—
Windmills, eateries, global awards,
Celebreties, software and soap.

SOLEMNITY AMONG THE RELICS

The well to the scaffold that stood
In the portico of the Bargello in Florence
Provided twenty-one basketfuls
Of bones. Upstairs, Donatello's
David stands on Goliath's dripping
Head. Saintly George is in armour.
In glass cases along the loggia
Repeated crucifixions rival
Papal fans to chase the flies
From the altar during holy mass.
Dante's deathmask infernally stares.

     Descending the staircase I looked up.
There she was in the mullion window
Two storeys high her face of joy
In consummation mocking me.

HONG KONG

The uncut ruby in Hong Kong
Substituted by tailored clothes
And fitted shoes.

In the outer harbour, burned, on her side,
Derelict there she lies,
The liner *Elizabeth*.

Twist the kaleidoscope...

LATEST REPORTS

The seasons of the tilted world come round again.
In March the brilliant crested scarlet cardinal
On the topmost branch of the bare-leaf apple tree—
Lakes from the glaciers—poets without
Sorrow, makers—may them come again
With all the answers—how many thousands of mites
Of infertility ride on the hummingbird's
Beak to the pouting blood-red lips of the Hamelia
Flower which they smell to get off to eat the pollen
And make love—what of the meanwhile historic
Cliff engravings threatened by the hyrdo dam
Of pragmatic Portugal? The shaky truce in the Balkans?
Heterogeneous conglomerates amalgamate.

NEAR THEBES

The valley rose to Parnassus, the home
Of the Muses, a place of wild trees
And clear waters near Grecian Thebes
Where Narcissus plunged in the artful pool
In love with his reflection.

                  I filched a pebble,
Souvenir of the spoiled richness.

THE SOPHISTICATED TRAVELLER

Culler of cathedrals, mosaics on walls,
Altamira, Dubrovnic, Uppsala,
Samarkand, Bangkok, Cairo,
D'Orsay on the winding Seine,
Elitist, nowhere else will do.

Constant rain fell on the metropolis,
The Boulevard bounced, the Deux-Magots
Café huddled, my socks were sloshed.
So it was, four days together,
Paris in March—where extravagant gardens
Grow, Cézanne's on tablecloths,
Van Gogh's Provençal poppies.

Winds from Aklavik came down
On provincial Québec four nights together,
My shoes were sloshed. Pneumonia caught
In Paris is much to be preferred.

Disharmonies

THE "LURKING ABYSS"

—EINSTEIN

Imperfection intervenes.
God is jealous, the ubiquitous devil
Set loose so good could be. One dies
Unfinished, irony enough for any
Day let alone Ash Wednesday.

And if after all there isn't anything,
Solvent death and nothing there,
Nothing at all, Saint Andrew lopsided,
Twitching Torquemada frustrated?

AT THE END THERE IS NO OTHER WAY

There is a blemish of dark along the snow,
Along the edge of the road where the field
Is. I have never seen the night
As dark, starless.

I turn, to the doorway to the house,
The light on in the doorway
Over the snow. There is time enough
Surely to do this?

FLOWERS FOR EASTER

The cosmos a mathematical equation.
Yet sadness persists—that striving
For the hereafter where nothing else will do.

Clouds are clouds. Faith, for the restless.

She walked the length of Wolfe Street
To the church to arrange flowers for the altar,
Logic no threat to Sunday, acceptable.
Design! The sadness persists.

    Suffering the means to get there.
    Adieu, forêts, Jeanne d'Arc's domain,
    Rough Peter's scriptural bait, the catch
    Considerable, Saint Matthew's tax collected.

THE TWISTER

And of disaster
Natural as the need to kneel
What shall be said?
God distributes contradiction.
The National Service early that morning
Broadcasts the warning:
The twister has grounded!
This was at Piedmont, northeastern
Alabama, on Palm Sunday.
The children were giving their play
"Watch the Lamb" in the Goshen
Methodist Temple. They huddled for safety,
Even as Jesus long ago rode
His easter out in Jerusalem.
The roof and windows blew apart,
The bonding mortar shattered!
The walls of the church came tumbling down.
Six children died. "Come unto Me,"
They say the saying is.

The system moved into Georgia.

EARLY INCIDENT

"Go climb it then," I cried,
Referring to the mountain. We were on an Oxford
Vacation. Of faith unconquerable, he later
Was a biship of the Church of England in Canada.
There it was, the Zugspitze
Of Garmisch-Partenkirchen in Bavaria
Made into a pilgrim's progress by him
As a way to heaven. We had climbed it
The day before, roped in
With strangers, the eternal glory of the sun,
A range of snowy crests to get to——
Trust in our shoes, crampons and mountain
Axe, guided, safe, with enough light
Left to be got down by.
"Faith is an ignorance," I said again,
The overtopping grin on his face
Irritating me. He was alright
But accepting—intelligent but leaning
On Mary's corpse somewhere up there
In the vicinity of Cancer in the zodiac.
I was half in bed and worn out
By the proposition of how could I prove
The unjust world confirmed Him
And the heavenly abode as non-existent.
I mentioned being born blind
And equivalents, geological massacres
Leading at the least to blackmail if not
To carelessness. No use. I put out
The light. "I will," he said in response
To my directive. I dreamed all night
Of angels ascending and descending ladders
Depsite the heavenly attested wings.

MEDITATION ABOUT BEING CONTINUOUS

Persistence is the only progress. I know
What it is, I have been brought low,
Pain a summer's length, yet October
As if I hadn't been put through it.
Stopping in the middle of tomorrow at the best
Is sorry business, Keats, Schubert,
Caeser stabbed, the Gulf War,
Vesuvius knowing when to blow.

     In Seville that Easter they carried the Virgin
In procession. Everyone knelt—the effigy
A dolled up doll with lights around
Her head run by batteries. The tourist
Next to me muttered "Oh God!"
But the cheapness paid off. To hundreds.
The procession goes on each year,
Don Quixote mistaken, windmills
Grind wheat that makes bread.
Bullfights are an ingrained aberration.
Hurt is one thing, loaves another.

     However that is, persistence
Makes sense, take it or leave it.
Than leave it I'd rather take it, the panoply
Of total stars over my head—
What we have is never conclusive.

SEPTEMBER

The leaves fall like rain,
A light wind and they fall.
There is no stop.

No more the foliage of simple
Things, time's place
Within the heart.

Across the farther green
Where winter's hemlocks edge
The uphill road,

I keep looking. Wherever
I look, each certainty is
As leaves fall to rest.

IN MEMORIAM

I

FOR A POET

Hot axe-heads put around
The neck and the tongue pulled out.
Poor Brebeuf!
Pratt remembering the Iroquois,
Ned annotating the flames.
What did it get you, old friend?
Erasure.

2

FOR A MAKER

From the bed he asked her to open the window,
He liked to hear the moonlight slanted
On the river. When she turned back
He was dead. John Walsh, designer
Of books. Forty-nine years.
The irony might have been less pointed,
Opening a window, serving poetry?

3

ELEGY FOR JEAN

May when the buds should come.
This year was a cold year,
Spring held back. The crocus
And the ground-phlox refused
To come.

Oh I do not wonder,
Thoughts of her down the street
Who painted three nuns
Staring in wonder at
A rose.

IT IS I SUPPOSE PROFOUNDLY SAD

Inherent irony, yes, yet strategy
To respond with, cancellation, anger—
While we last—at night, those stars,
A conquest of them, a thousand city
Windows smashed by the morning sun.
Imbalance. Yet as far as we
Could go, the North Cape, not
A sunset to complain of.
At The Hague the widower, the old man
Sitting by the water's edge
Content, knowing he had made it,
Love, he explained, the crowd going by
At noon. Underground in Kiev's
Monastery the pile of pious skulls
To balance the brain—that revised me!
But God loves that, the sleight
Of hand, what you don't think will happen,
The ambiguity of being born,
The suffering to get rid of this bone-house
We walk around with, the child's
First ball bounced under
The last decadence of the incipient moon.

Strategy?

AMBIVALENCE

God threw the dice and let nature
Work itself out. A silly gesture unless
He was bored (that use of the capital "H"
Because we can't seem to do without
Him—the beginning of a line takes a capital,
A convenient subterfuge to duck asserting
Conclusive Divinity). Darwin or God still
The flaring debate. Are all insects small,
The inevitable result of their lack of bony skeletons?
Or part of the grand Purpose? A fiat to keep
Ant-eaters and frogs from taking over?

      What? I sit and listen to the songster on the bough
Of the crab apple tree, thankful for its skeleton.

DECISION

How in God's name I ever took on
God, God knows, a silliness to erase,
The world set straight if he can
And hasn't quit the whole idea
And left man to his own devices,
It's more than he can handle and God
Too if my guess is right—innocence
Suffering, disaster, plague. Yes,
I remember Job, also eight hundred
Drowned in his recent turbulent seas,
Five thousand when the earth shook.

     The cosmos not quite finished? Faith
More than justice? Eden, an offhand
Prohibition?

     I'll have nothing to do with
Anything beyond the speed of light.

SENSUALITIES

i
The lioness gnaws
On the gazelle—
The leg still quivering.

The hummingbird
That ate nectar
Is brought in the cat's mouth
To where I sit.

ii
The hibisus blossom
Lasts two days at most
Stamen stiff
Offering seed.

iii
The two white birches,
One root when it was planted,
Shed stripped bark.

Fold your hand around.
Insist.

iv
Rinse your hands at the faucet
For the outdoor garden hose,
The contact, if you can take it,
Ice-cold.

v

Daffodils stiff against the amorous wind,
Fooling the bee with sweet illusion—
God! how the damp earth smells
And March wind slaps the cheek with cold!

EQUIVALENCE

Men step in their coffins without shoes
Disliked or not,
The room at last theirs.

Houses rise up among the district poor,
Sometimes compassion.
We are all possibilities.

THE SLANTING SEA

The whales sang each to each the day
We watched. A safe distance from the harbour
Leaps split blue. We landed
After hours. There they still were
On the church steps, the mendicants,
A hand cut off at the wrist for theft,
Passion stoned, obeisance four
Times for Paradise, a tooth for a tooth.
Across the turbulent seas, Buddha
Impassive, a footprint in indelible rock,
Celebrants of risen corpses in heaven.

The whales leaped in grace where
They lived in the slanting sea.

ARGUMENT BOTH WAYS

Until I get the hang of it, crucifixion
Will be without metaphors, no godly
Interjection applying concern,
Bodies benign, cows chawing,
Mankind ploughing, reversals corrected,
Everyone minding his own business
Having supper, hurting no one.

      The last I had was at the Chinese
Restaurant in British Columbia, no Judas
To spoil it—seven poets, mostly,
Sweet and sour pork, chicken
Cashew, rice, my idea
Of a menu though bread and wine will do.
God would approve, it seems to me.

IMPASSE

Thrust of impasse as if never planned for—
The Rocky Mountains across the harvest plains.

     The Chevrolet, hand-wound gramophone, records,
Irrelevant books, piled in the back,
At the end of the driving day we faced
Heights, sunsets on the mountains,
Sunrise. Omission never thought of.

        We fed the deer at Wapta Falls,
        Sat by the open fire, pans,
        Coffee pot, done-with—ahead of us,
        Metaphors, glaciers, passes; across
        The vastness, solitude defined.

        We climbed Yoho, Revelstoke,
        Crossed fields of flowers,
        Our minds on uplands.
        Ability was commencement,
        Poor-boxes, candle-ends,
        Forgotten.

Apportioned Love

ASSERTION

Harmony or disharmony under the aegis
Of heaven, I'd go through the whole thing over again,
Error, heavenly fumbling still to be corrected,
Children somewhere else in sufferance, defective
Birth, Down's syndrome too usual to find
A place on the news hour and prime-time of prayer,
Yet Venus up there still beautiful
Spinning in the night! Painted by Botticelli.

      I have known a few
      Adults who are grown up.

   You trust my saying this, don't you?
   Of course you do, raising your glass
   Sitting there in affirmation.

APPORTIONED LOVE

No, it won't do, extinction,
Inevitable impoverishment, I won't accept it—
If I could—still there is Beethoven's
Mythical clenched fist at the final
Thunder; rage at the thirty pieces
Of silver.

       Prayer in the lonely nave
Be what it has to—an end to the debate!
Brevity accepted though moths eat the clothing
(Did you feel that chill?), whatever abstraction
Is, without injustice, time's
Endurable no matter God's ambition.

EACH KNOWS OF IT

Whatever distractions to be observed,
Temperament save the world. Haydn
Loved wit as much as heaven;
Aunt Emma on my father's side
Loved goldfish; there are grandchildren,
Rock-candy! What the solution
Is, not the only business.

     "O Absalom, my son, my son!"
"No, no, no life."
Passion, poetry; Mother Teresa
Bending down. Respect for all of it!
A man fishing, a woman ironing.
Grandeur, each knows of it.

SCENARIO

Nature insists. At last report
The geese came home, warmed their eggs,
Acknowledged the contents; penguins waddled
Up the populous beach; the ozone
Puncture responded to muzzled smokestacks.
One day traffic stopped dead
And watched the barefoot gathering shove
The stranded whale back to sea.
Happiness descended! Squawling infants!
Fathers stayed home to enjoy them. On the prairies
Tractors sewed what is useful. Ancient
Incontrovertible documents attest it.

EXCLUSION

I can remember when I paid homage
To a stream found in the woods,
Before computers took over,
Wonder still calculable and profit
Not in it except to be kept quiet about.

I stand on the grassy knoll near there
Unfazed and let out my breath.
Affirmation tugs my sleeve.

THERE ARE SURPLUSES

That the good Cemetery Association
Should send me a reminder that I owe
Remembrances, renewed plants
And flowers on the graves of my parents
Is understandable but no less at the moment
Out of keeping, northern shadows
In the crusts of snow are ineffectual,
Past sorrows are out of line,
Consistencies have to be sorted out,
Festivals of music are announced
In foreign cities...

                 Remembrances
Look after themselves pretty well.
I have arranged permanent decencies.
Resilience is possible.

WHAT HAPPENED

Ceremony is an advantage
Like a placed comma.

Gin-and-bitter-lemon
Was first that first night
At the Oak Room of the Plaza.
She knew music, the exchanges
Covered the room's three
Duplicate dining prologues.
Then chicken-à-la-king,
Sunset barely admissable.
Rhythm and theme as in music
Set the substance, fact
As in poetry got meaning.
Central park was next,
The Tavern on the Green
Where hackneys no longer go.

Authenticity took over
The next forty years.

YOU WOULDN'T DREAM IT COULD BE DONE

The sea otter lies on his back
And cracks open a clam—old
Sad eyes and whiskers, slim grey
In the sliding ocean.

He's in mortal danger of course.
Sharks love him. But there he is
Opening clamped clams on his back
In the middle of the problem.

WATER MUSIC

George III bathed off Weymouth
To the accompaniment of a chamber orchestra.
No idiot he. With brains and money
Near the seaside, we'd all do it,
Dunking, dipping to the bass fiddles
Of Beethoven's *Eroica*!
"Ja, and the Yankee States disloyal!"
Hart Crane dived out of life
From the rolling deck of the *Orizaba*.
But he was mixed up. He didn't
Listen to Schubert's *Trout Quintet*.

      O to swim to the portentous tuba,
Ride the waves to the fiddling flute!

PERSONAL CHAMBER MUSIC

I knew I was alive when
I preferred Milhaud's
"La Création du Monde"
To Beethoven's "Grosse Fugue."
What weariness has brought me to!
And welcome—
With double for Poulenc's
"Trio for Piano, Oboe, and Bassoon,"
Plugged-in instruments
Out in left field.
Sad but there it is.

      Hark—not the *herald angels sing*—
Poulenc potters amongst the keys!

INTERMISSION (PASTORALE)

"A few minutes refreshment for the weary soul."
So it was when Haydn wrote, and so
It is for the sheer burning colour of the cardinal
Come from the south to shuffled summer. So
It is, the wooden bucket in the yard hung
Over the well-water smackingly cold,
The unchangeable sun above. After the divergent
Day, so it is, the silence of the poem.

As Before

HERITAGE

The promise of the morning is what we had.
Appalachian hills, the house,

Lime Ridge where the Junction was,
Mirror Lake, the commercial road,

The covered bridge that was winter solved,
Burgeoning summer over with,

Wisdom enough for coming seasons.
The years that generations served

Hostage to harvest weather,
Full garners, eventual token,

The crabapple left, the fieldfence broken.
I stand still at the railway cutting

Hammering fool's gold, iron pyrites!
And yet not so unwise, the heart's

Schooling. The attic. Under the gable
The albums closed and kept, boxes,

Tomorrows still assignable,
Yesterdays their own bequest.

Heritage! Trust returned-to,
The land, occasional, never left.

THE GATHERER

Forthright, as the scythe
To the standing grain, he pauses,
The dusk the last
Of the northern August sun.

Tomorrow clear, the western sky
Rich to the promise not yet done.
The cattle wait
At the barred wooden close,

The whole of the world waits
The future of his stroke.
The last songbird
Stops. He hangs the scythe.

The silo on the upward road is framed
In the barn doorway; at the bruised basin
Cold runs,
Harsh at his elbow.

NEW YEAR'S NIGHT

The red scarf and tuque with the pompon on it
Rounds hither and skelter on the rigorous rink
Beneath the moon. The small boy and the girls
Have them a time as lively as Haydn's
B-flat *finale*—Count Apponyi commissioned
Half a dozen quartets for the Austrian Court—
Kids on skates on the Capelton rink as gay
As that—the house chimneys under the stars,
The holiday kids on skates going circles
Aware of deserving nothing, only now.

AS SEEN FROM DUFFERIN HEIGHTS

An obviously stupid creature by the look
It gives one if disturbed by a sound
As it sits legs folded under
On the upland meadow, the background
Of Lake Massawippi and the Champlain
Valley in Vermont breathtaking
If you have the sensitivity for it,
The cows chewing cud there
Offering a very necessary product
As grass-green poets do.

IN THE BACK GARDEN

A good clutch of the hind legs
Around the outer portion of the petal
And a push inside for nectar,
That is the curriculum to follow.

I watched the bee do it, bees
Without a thought who work on instinct
Which brains curtail. Genetic genius
Very rare in the human kingdom.

Brains can be beneficial, philosophy
Sorting out scrambling aesthetics.
But perhaps not. Not these days,
Soap and celebrity the ultimate goal.

One should mention that young man
Of Nazereth, a pretty good carpenter by trade
Who put two wooden planks together.
Luckless though. I tell you what:

Brains and instinct both, each
In the right proportion: an open toasted
Hearth and carpet slippers for instinct,
Irreducible experience for brains.

EARLY MORNING SPONTANEITY

Hoodwinked, the mind asleep,
Health fooled me.
I shoved aside the blanket,
Stretched my immortal soul.

The need for worship led me on.
Bone through the nose,
The fire ablaze, the circlers stomped,
The asked-for god came down.

Six days he took to set
The cosmos up,
Choice set free.
How could He know?

Miracles only heal the flesh,
The cripple on the roadside
The stumbling done, Lazarus
Come to tell of death

While sainthood drops its alm!
A sad world, sad.
The jester gave all he had,
Hardwon grace:

Clothed in motley, stood on his hands
In the chancel, the holy
Candles upside down.
God sustains the flaw.

Alas, alas, too much to know.
I pull on my briefs,
Tie my shoes, go down
The stricken bedroom stairs.

CONCLUSIONS FROM SMALL SOURCES

1

The fat bird sits
on the limb of the bare lilac-bush
picking underwing lice.
The squirrel eats the seeds
spread out for beautiful birds.

The mixture of the universe
is not romantic.

2

The wheezy siskin clutches
on the winter branch.
The cardinal
whose colour without putting
his mind to it
causes halt of breath,
waits for the invisible sap.

3

The elongated poplar
which threatened to fall on the house
is cut down.
The majestic hunks
suggest cinnamon.

4
I thought to disentangle
    frost from flower,
the spider spins decision
    appropriately,
whereas the impact
    determines conclusion.

POETRY ITSELF THE PROGENITOR

What, shall we sit and think again
Poetry into succession?
Yea—as they used to say.
The art had been done, I thought,
Turning weather whatever it is,
Into self-solution,
Hating my father, loving my father,
The sun goes up, the sun goes down.

Poetry!
The crux of it—
Fact shuffling off the stage,
Meaning wearing buskins on...
Outside the vestibule
Rain raining,
The loon across the lake
Crying the moon
Above the headstones.

How it is said
Is what it is.

You know what I mean?

Umbrellas raised in rinsing rain?

THE MORALITY OF POETRY

Sensation held to true account,
Thisness exacted, meaning in surmounting
Accuracy—words, each to each,
As time is as breathing is, as tide
Suggests the moon and obstinate stone
The Druids' haulings, Stephen martyred,
Though stone is stone, indurate, impassive,
Beyond harmonics, only itself.

    In poetry, a double allocation:
Depth and degree of breath, the meaning;
The rhythm right, let the metrics clash
As they will, rough or smooth,
What is meant is in the hearing,
How it is said, the true delight—
The termpering power the consummate heart—
Emotion alert for the vowel, the consonant's
Unobtrusive constancy:
Movement, resonance, one with silence!

    An ordering of accurate words
        Will do.

SOLUTION

The whole of the morning gone, thrown
Away. Inevitable noon.

All night the poem presented itself.
In vain. All is said.

Only the smell of the roasted coffee
Remains. Recycle my soul!

No one need know then,
Insufficient dawn!

EMPTY PRAYER AT THE END OF THE DAY

I should have been born a maker
      of cabinets
Smelling of pine,
      fitted pine.

I am acquainted with remoteness!
It should have been
      a lighthouse,
In seclusion.

December Poems

BLUE IS FOR THE SPLENDOUR

Two crows, harbingers of fate...
But the birds were blue (though the shadows filtered
The winter light; the sound of honey-bees
On the near clover long silent)
The flash of colour I saw was the right
Size—bluebirds? bluejays?

Parentheses stumble simplicity...
But double blue the birds were—
Double blue like my love.
I saw them from the hospital window
As they flew to the green conifer woods
In the fallen dusk, the colour distinguishable...

[December 6, 1994]

LYRIC

For those without relief except through death
I mourn. May all remembrances gather—
That hour, that day, the gift disencumbered.

In the crowded hospital corridor the suffering wait,
Eyes ask … God save us, above the hills,
Nine clouds, a living wonder! Count them.

[December 8th]

THE PURE DESIGN

Dying! Nothing but faith, the going
Without reason. I walk by the partly
Open doorway on the corridor.
He lay on his left side, twenty, thirty?
The hospital linen, the pillow, white,
The thermos of water and glass out of reach,
The blind of the window half drawn,
The slope and the spruce to be seen
If he turned. The third hour. I know
His surgeon slightly. Dying alone.

[December 12th]

POEM OF HUMOUR

Wasted humour! Movement to movement
Rhythms alter! The Bethlehem songs
Came from the corridor while I was troubled
Involuntarily. Six, six
Sweet voices. A piano accompaniment. "Hark!
Glory to the new-born King!"
Yes, out of order! Forgive us! The world
Worse, ourselves unreconciled.

[December 14th]

ON THE WATERS HE WALKED

While I slept in my hospital bed
From pain, someone I did not know
Placed out of time the fresh-spread sandwich
On the mobile table at my side.
Someone who could not stand the pain
In others, the answer I was inclined-to
Reading the sardonics of Wystan Auden
The English poet who had written
That nine-tenths of the living world
Is beyond a fracture no empathy
Can cross. Look elsewhere than around here
For your disillusioned increment
My empathetic salmon sandwich
Pronounced, more hungry than Biblical I preached,
Go fish the waters that He once walked!

[December 22nd]

IN THE BEGINNING WAS THE WORD

Alongside the Argyle road
The slant goes upward to the church.
The organ praised the Lord. The world
Went on, finishing and beginning,
The hospital quietly there. The mother
In Sunday best walked the boy,
The girl, to worship Good, one
Who lifelong did no hurt.

     Along the hall the Christmas patients,
Six of them, suffer affliction.

     I watched until the sermon ended.
The children free from her hand
Hurled snow. The mother saw me
At the window. Raised her hand.

     I had no answer. Though I waved.
My neighbour sang because his belly
Ached. A carol his mother taught him,
So he said. Perhaps compassion for the suffering?

[December 24th]

CHRISTMAS PROGRESSION

A huddle of empirical penguins in the Antarctic cold.
That's what they looked like, the group of nuns,
White robes blowing, possessing their beloved God.
Would I were of their wonder, believing only
In reason, imperfection.

                       In tribute they passed
Along the pathway into church. Blow
Your trumpet, Gabriel! The argument is done.
Singly they walk within, the valiance won.
The clanking bell in dissonance...

                              [December 25th]